W9-CAL-614

Bah, Humbug!

by

SCHULZ

CollinsPublishersSanFrancisco
A Division of HarperCollins Publishers

'Tis The Season To Be Selling

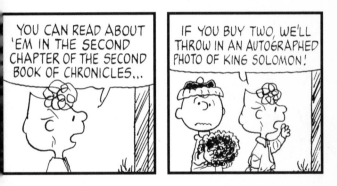

Christmas Cheer By Mail

Deck
The Malls...

LOOK, YOU CAN STILL SEE THE SLEIGH TRACKS IN THE SNOW...

AND THE HOOF PRINTS FROM THE REINDEER..SEE? RIGHT ALONG HERE...

AND NOW YOU CAN SEE WHERE THEY END...THIS IS PROBABLY WHERE THEY TOOK OFF INTO THE AIR...

HE REMEMBERED!

A Packaged Goods Incorporated Book
First published 1996 by Collins Publishers San Francisco
1160 Battery Street, San Francisco, CA 94111-1213
http://www.harpercollins.com
Conceived and produced by Packaged Goods Incorporated
276 Fifth Avenue, New York, NY 10001
A Quarto Company
Based on the PEANUTS ® comic strip by Charles M. Schulz
http://www.unitedmedia.com
Library of Congress Cataloging-in-Publication Number 96-14895
Bah, humbug! / by Schulz.
ISBN 0-00-225213-9

Printed in Hong Kong

1 3 5 7 9 10 8 6 4 2